This Coloring Book Belongs To:

....

Copyright notice:

Published by **POD ONLY Publishing**

Enjoy Your Coloring!

Without your input we don't exist.

Please, cheer us and leave a review!

Thank You!

Christmas is the day that holds all time together.

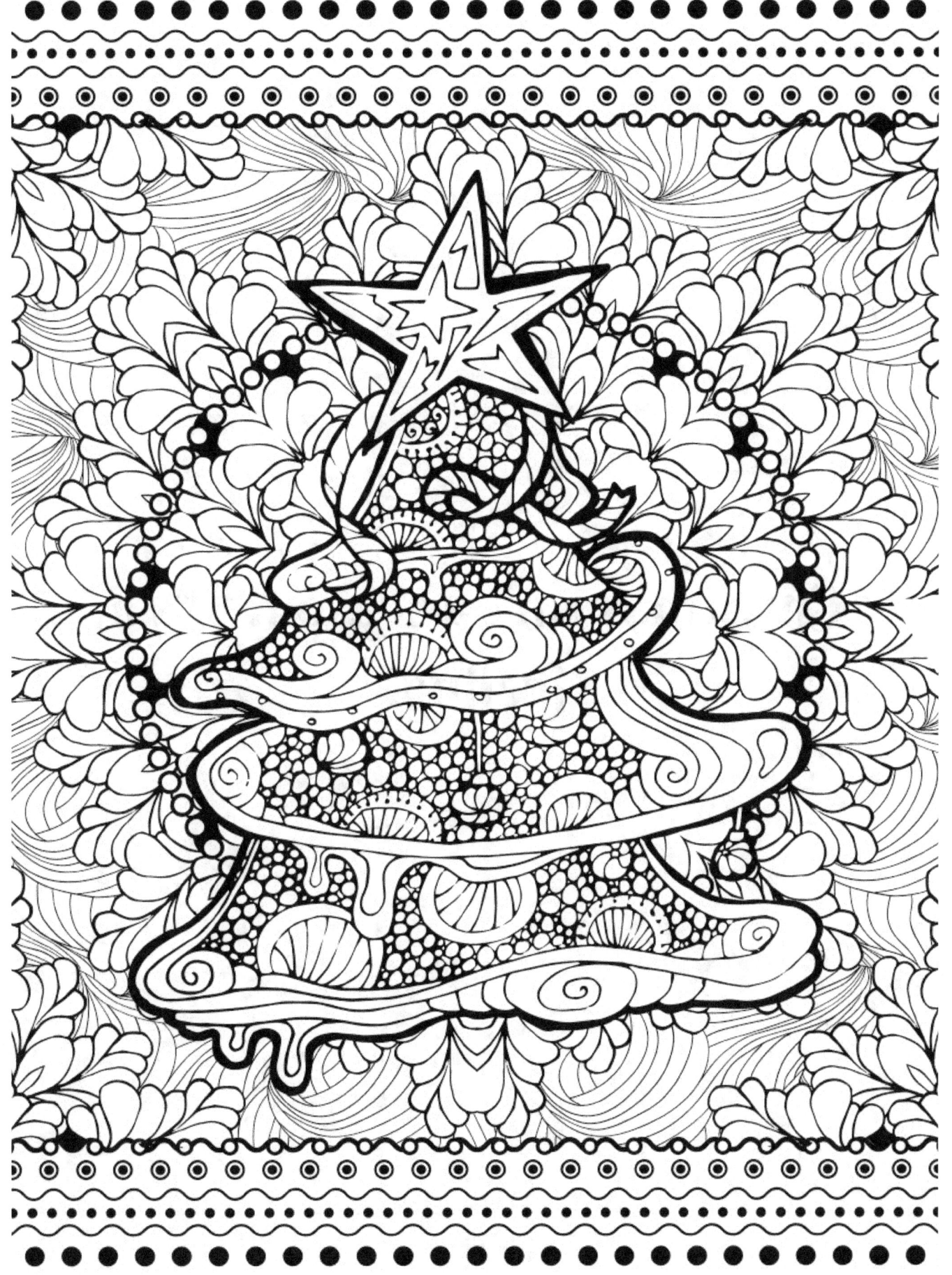

Christmas isn't a season. It's a feeling.

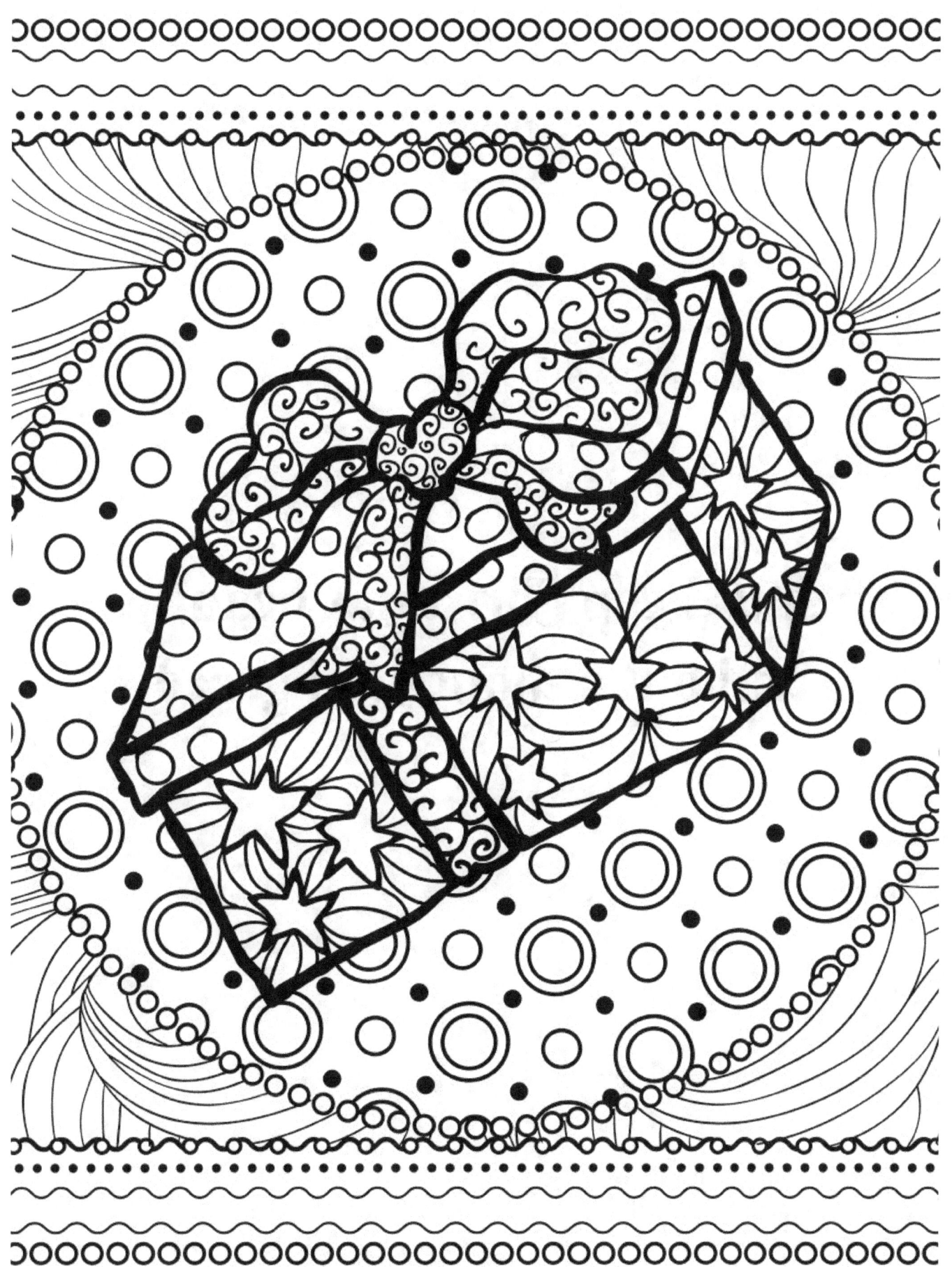

Let us keep Christmas beautiful without a thought of greed.

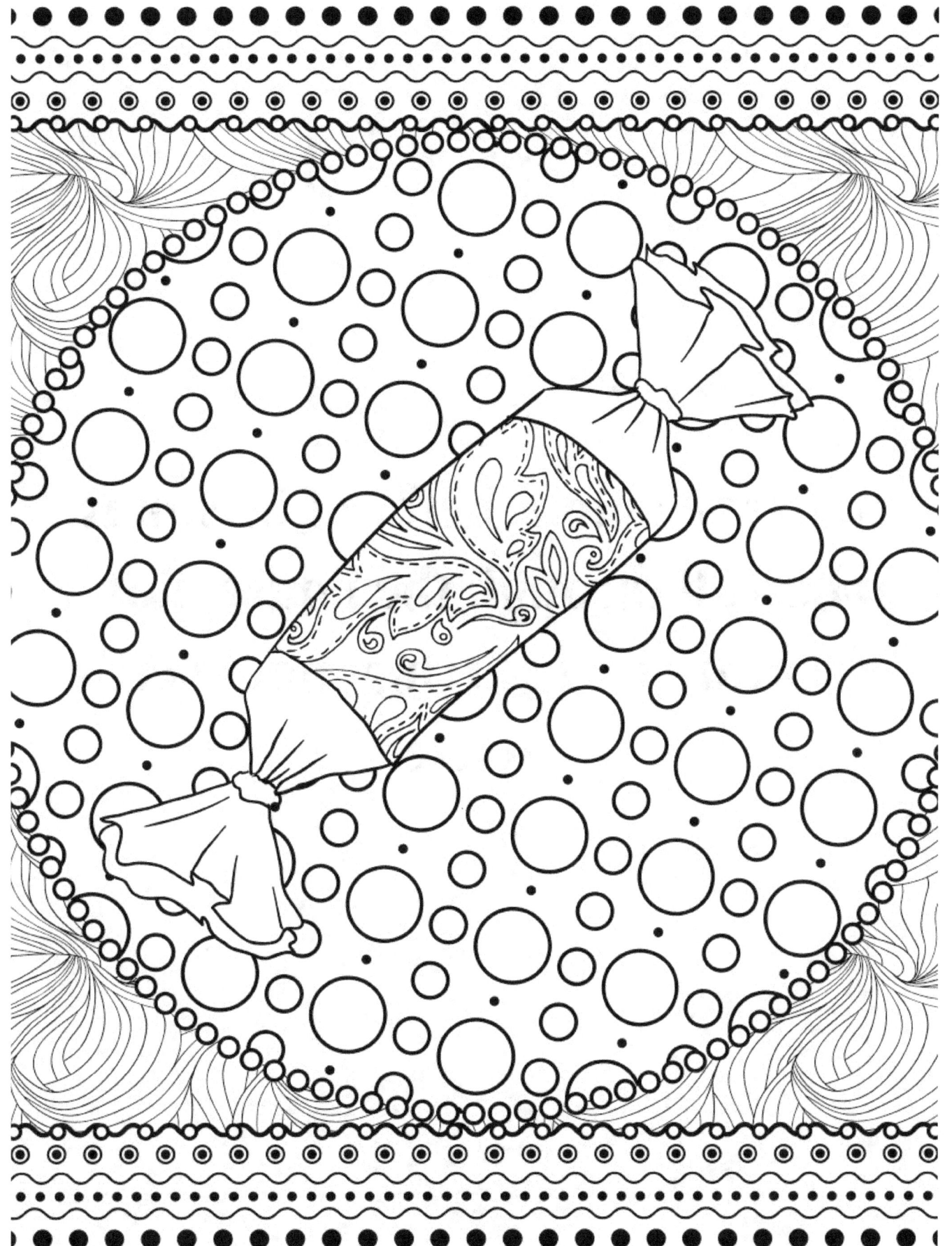

Twas the night before Christmas, when all through the house, not a creature was stirring, not even a mouse.

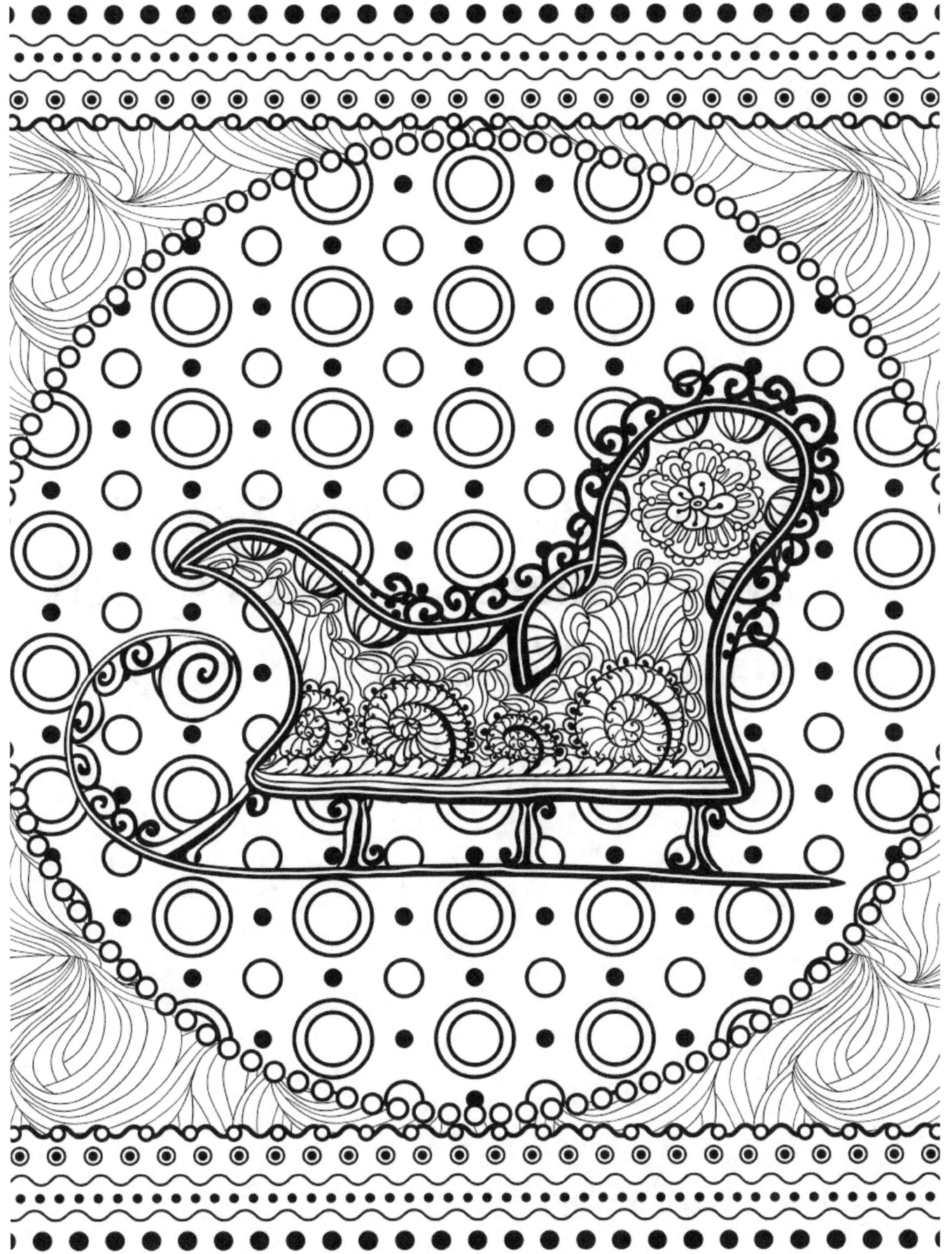

Unless we make Christmas an occasion to share our blessings, all the snow in Alaska won't make it 'white.'

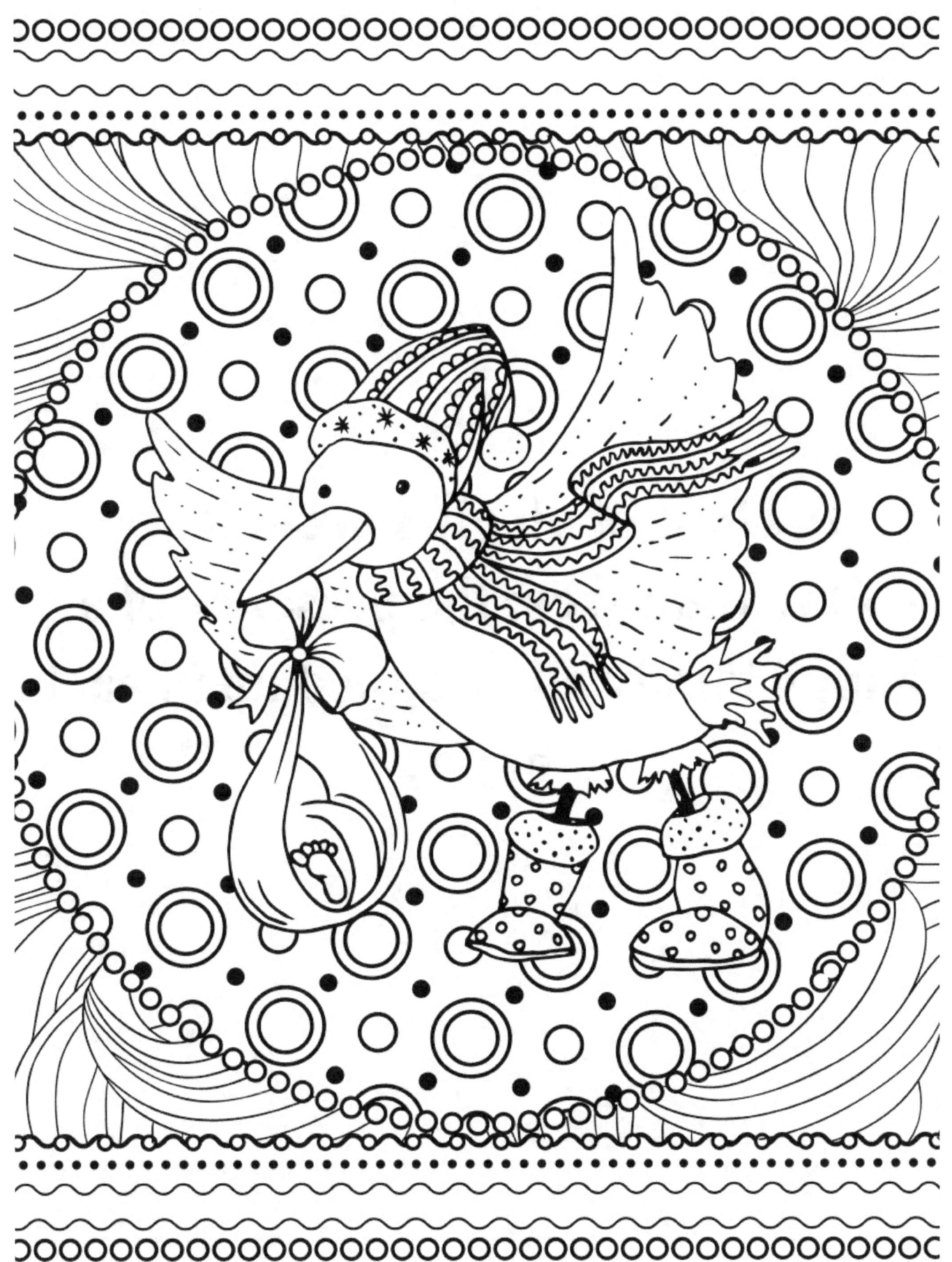

The best of all gifts around any Christmas tree: the presence of a happy family all wrapped up in each other.

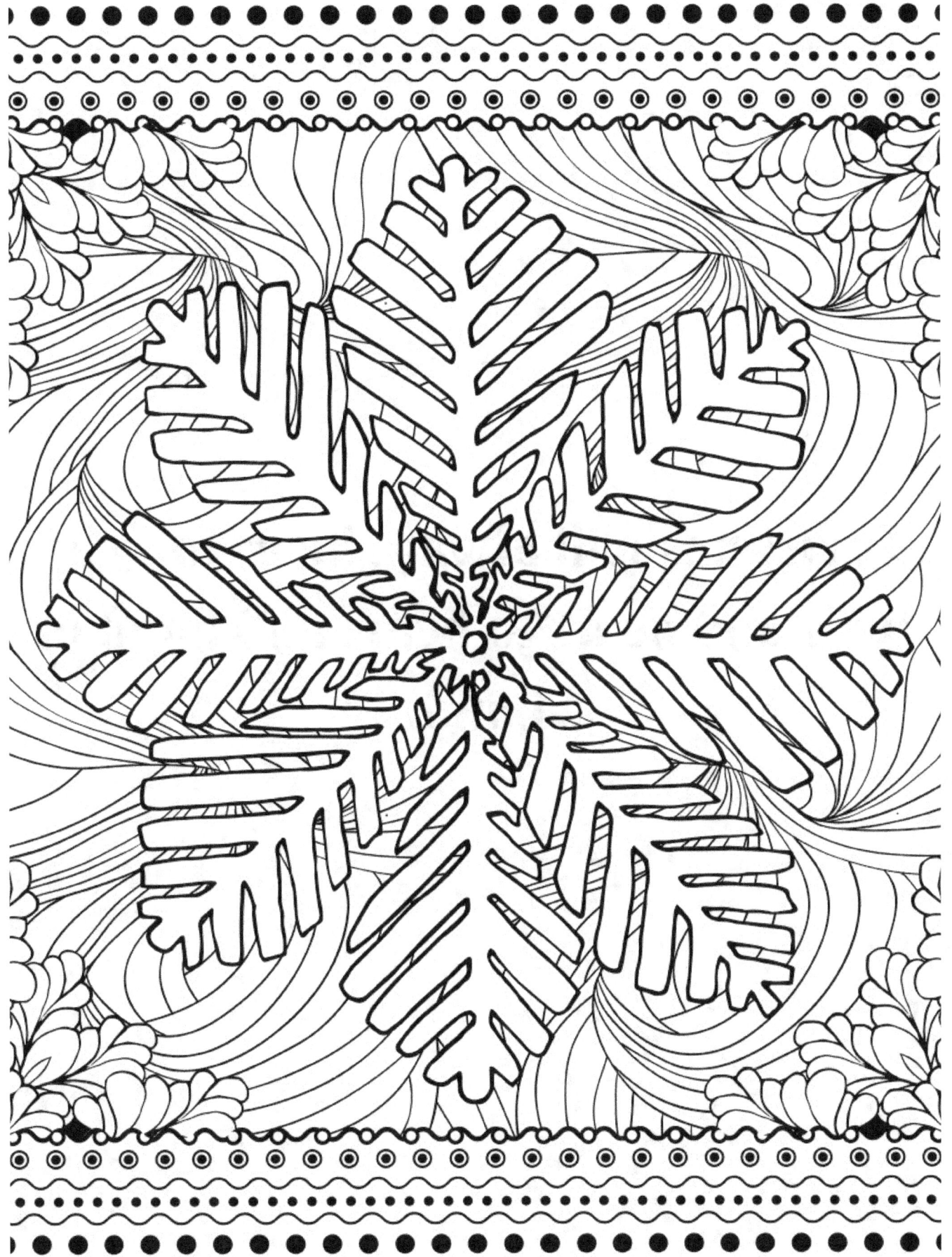

Christmas will always be as long as we stand heart to heart and hand in hand.

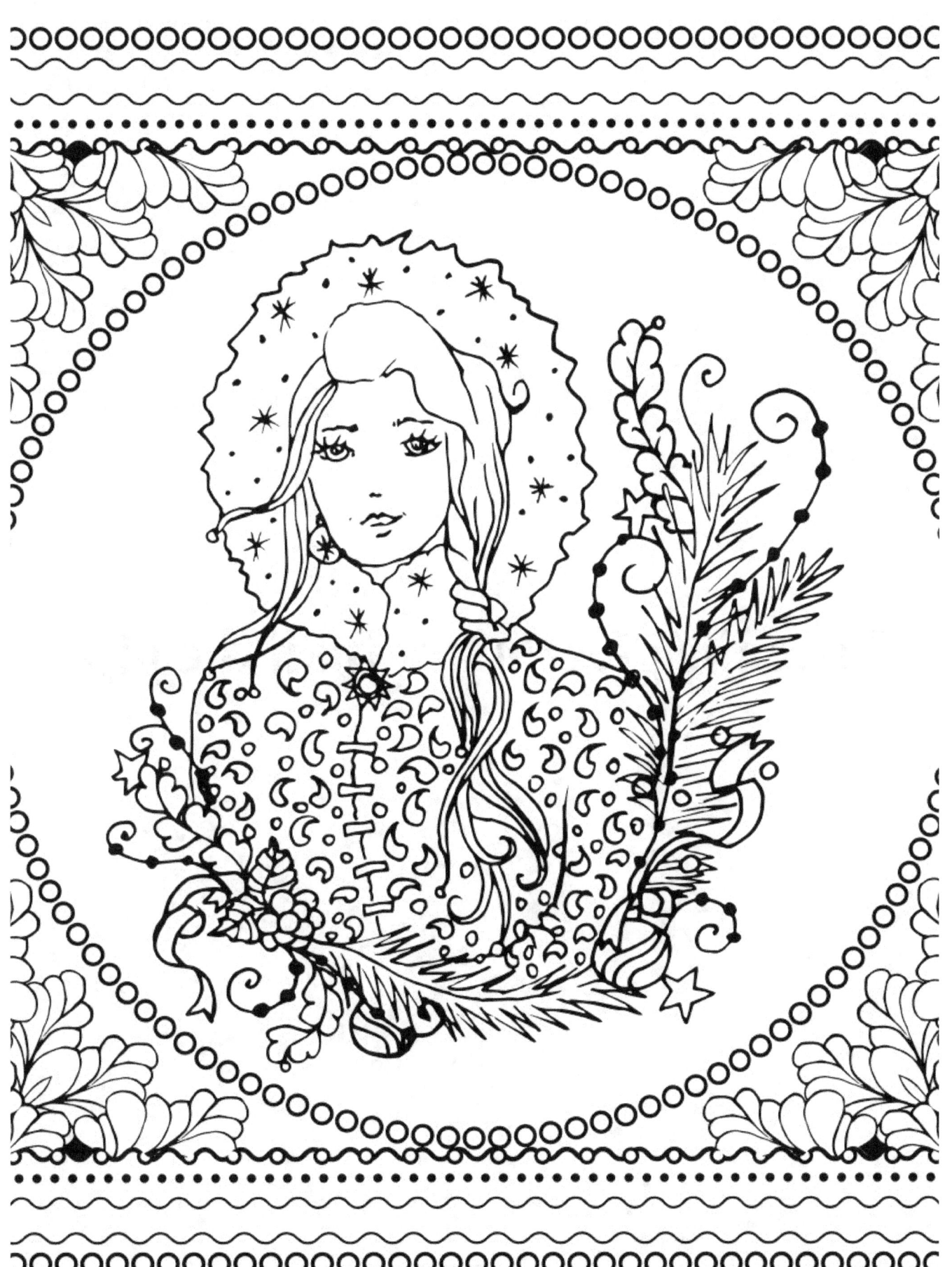

Love the giver more than the gift.

Christmas is a necessity. There has to be at least one day of the year to remind us that we're here for something else besides ourselves.

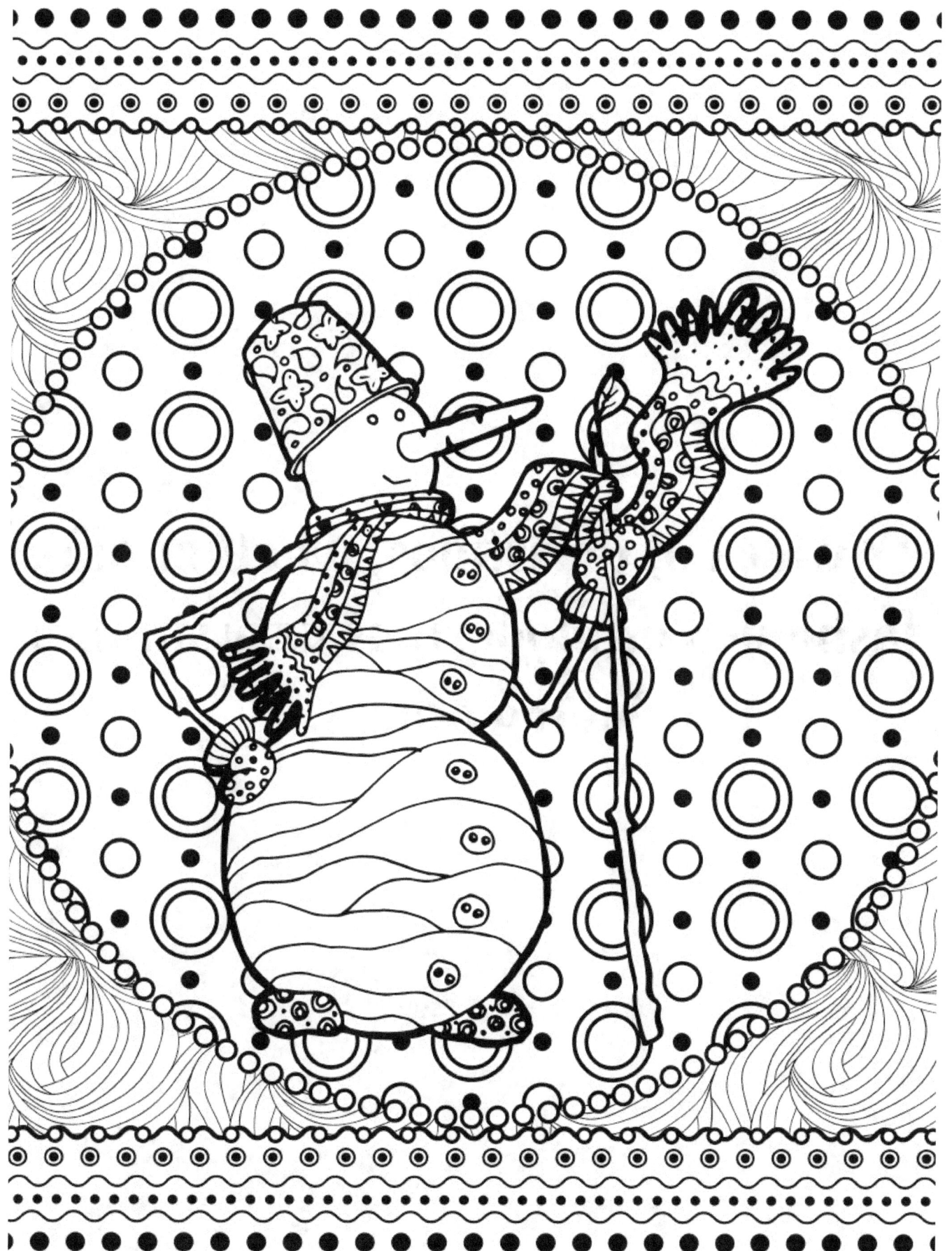

My idea of Christmas, whether old-fashioned or modern, is very simple: loving others.

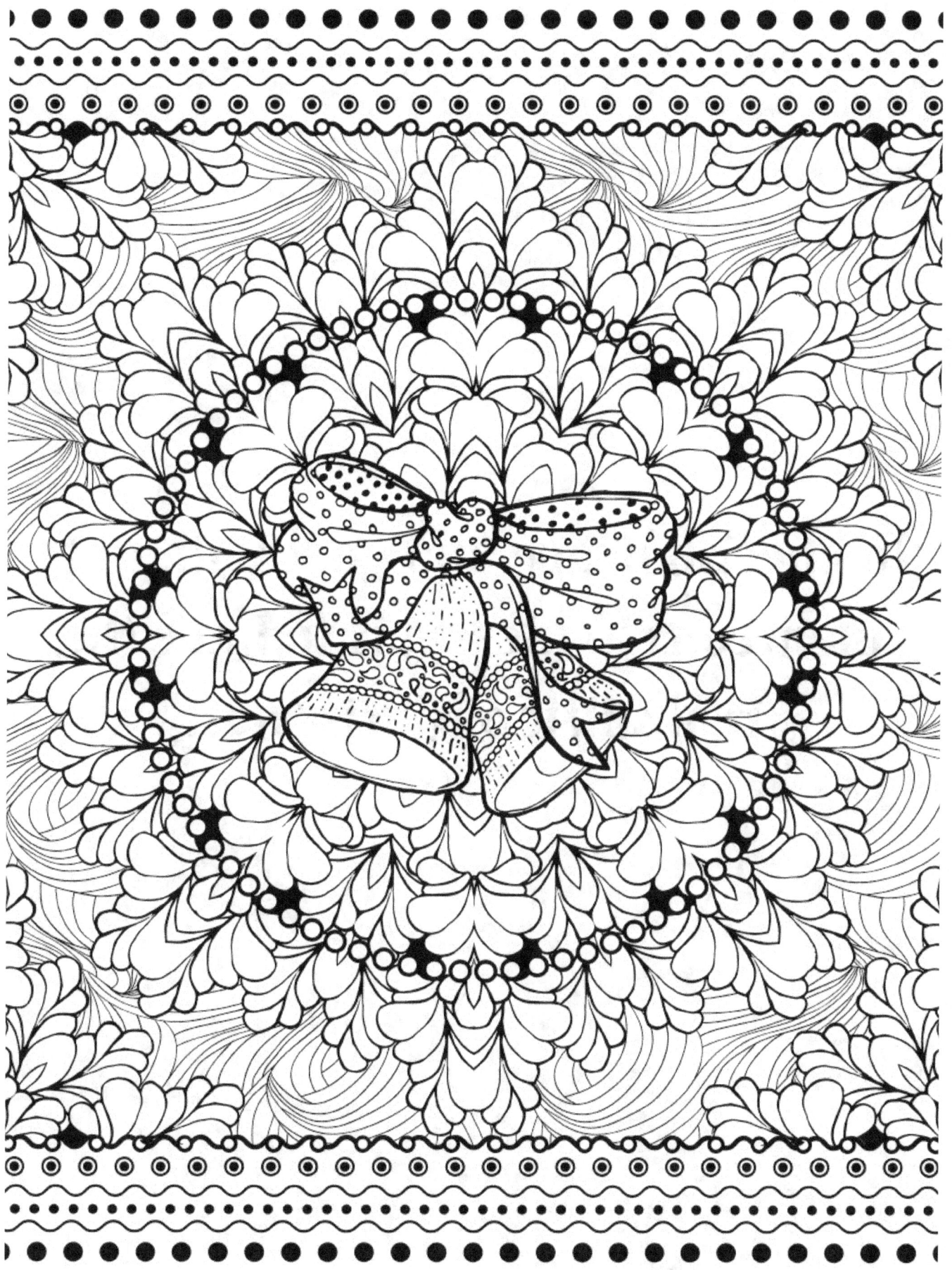

To cherish peace and goodwill, to be plenteous in mercy, is to have the real spirit of Christmas.

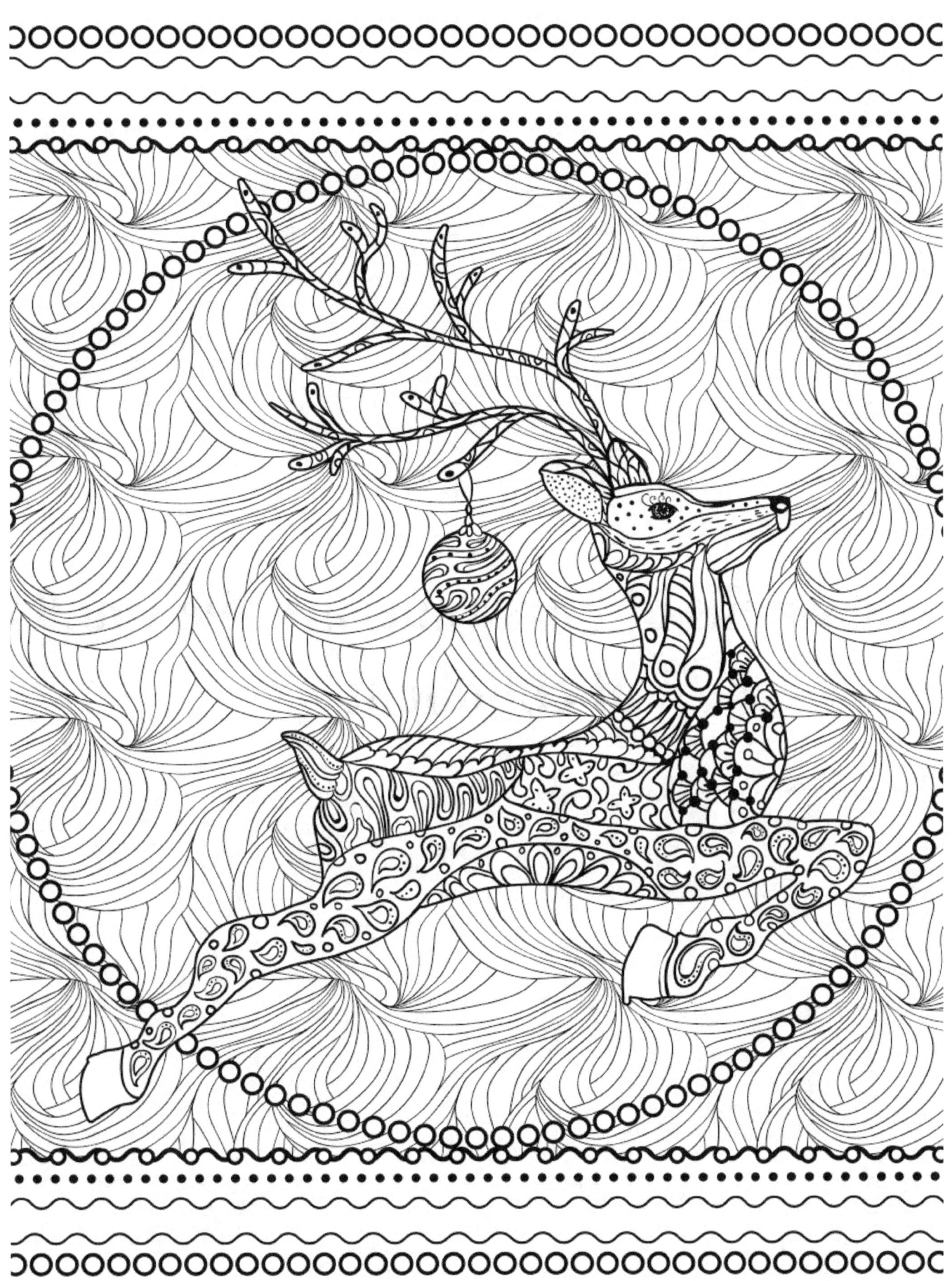

The smells of Christmas are the smells of childhood.

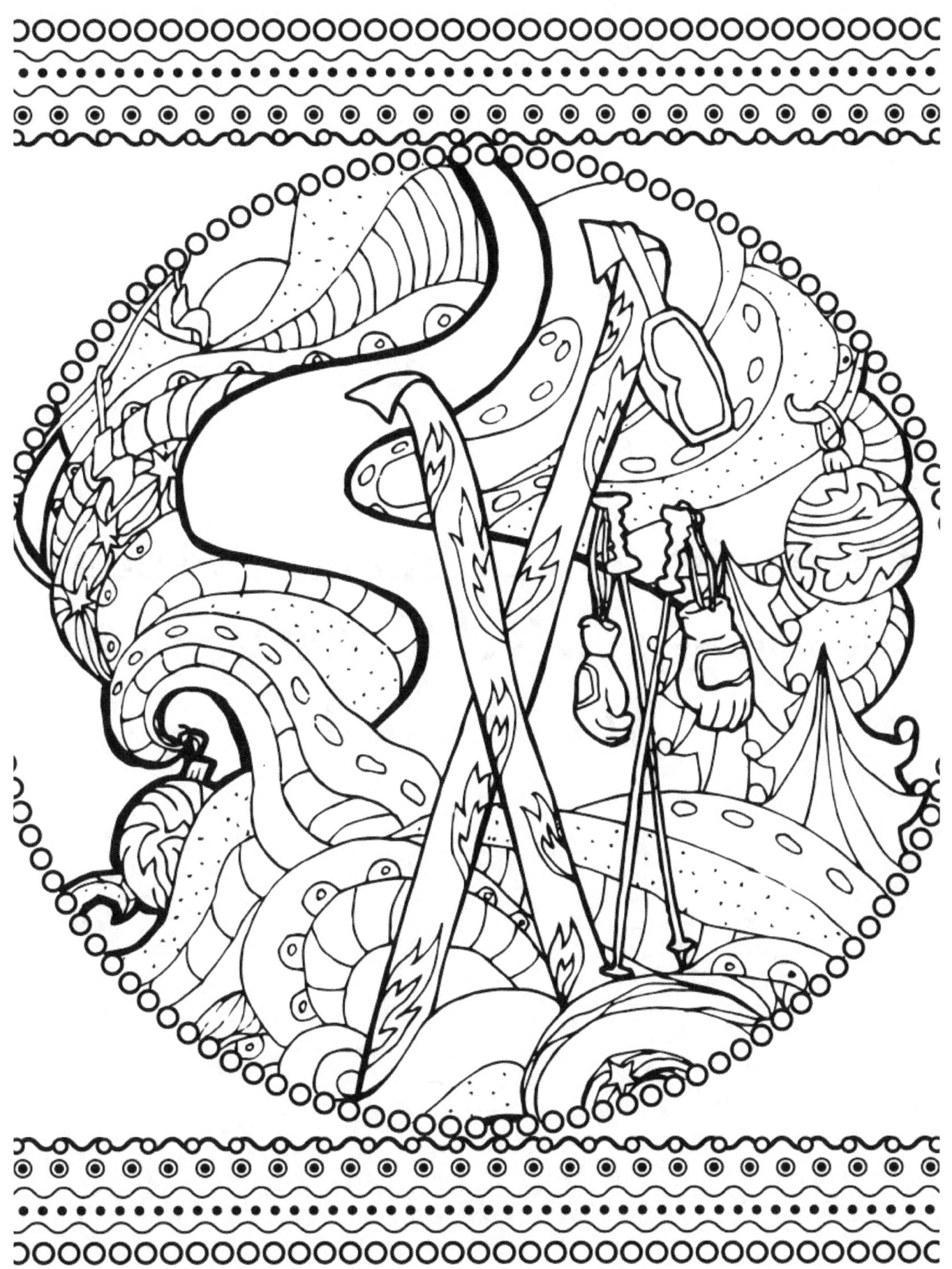

Christmas magic is silent. You don't hear it — you feel it. You know it. You believe it.

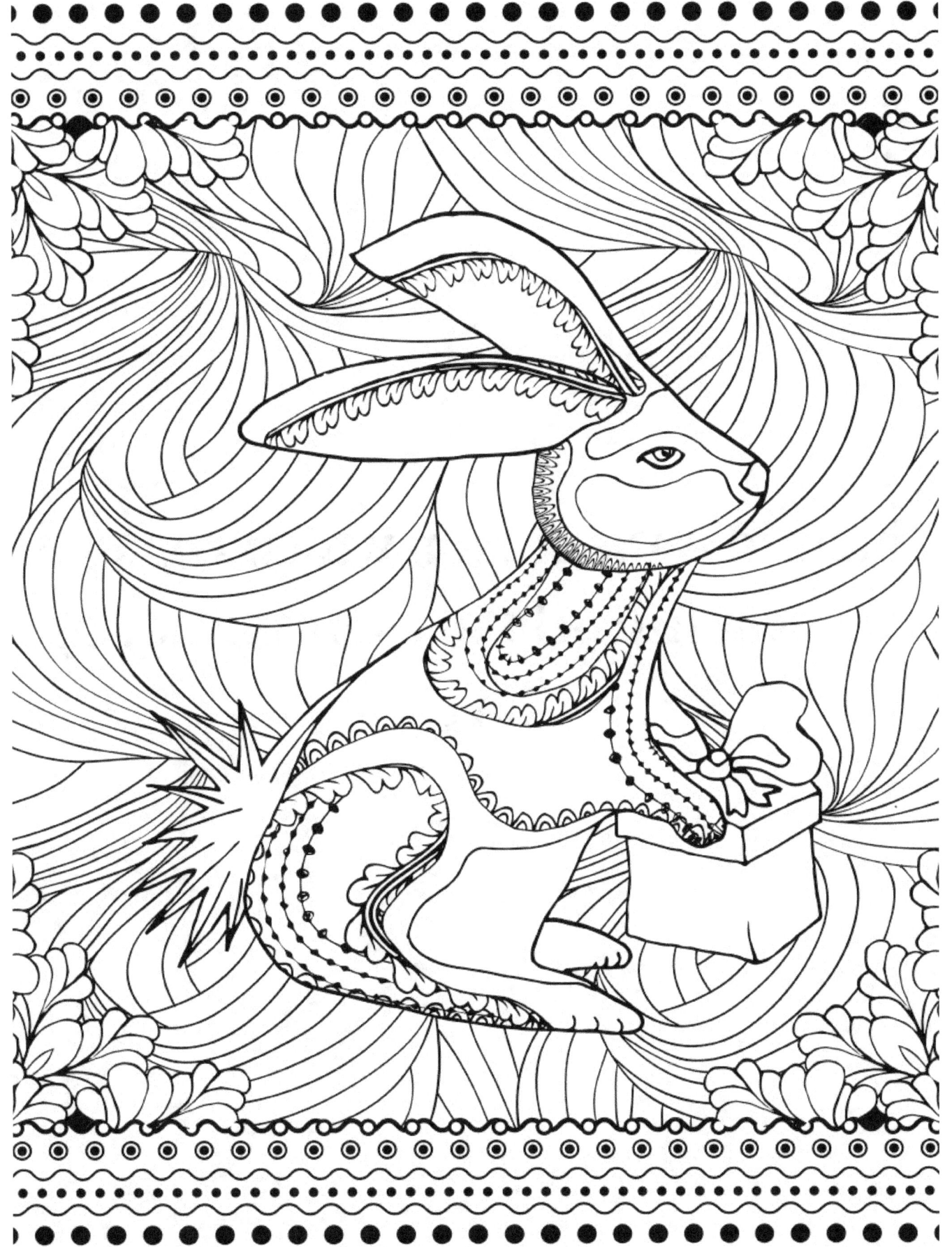

Blessed is the season which engages the whole world in a conspiracy of love.

Merry Christmas!

I don't think Christmas is necessarily about things. It's about being good to one another.

Christmas is a time when you get homesick — even when you're home.

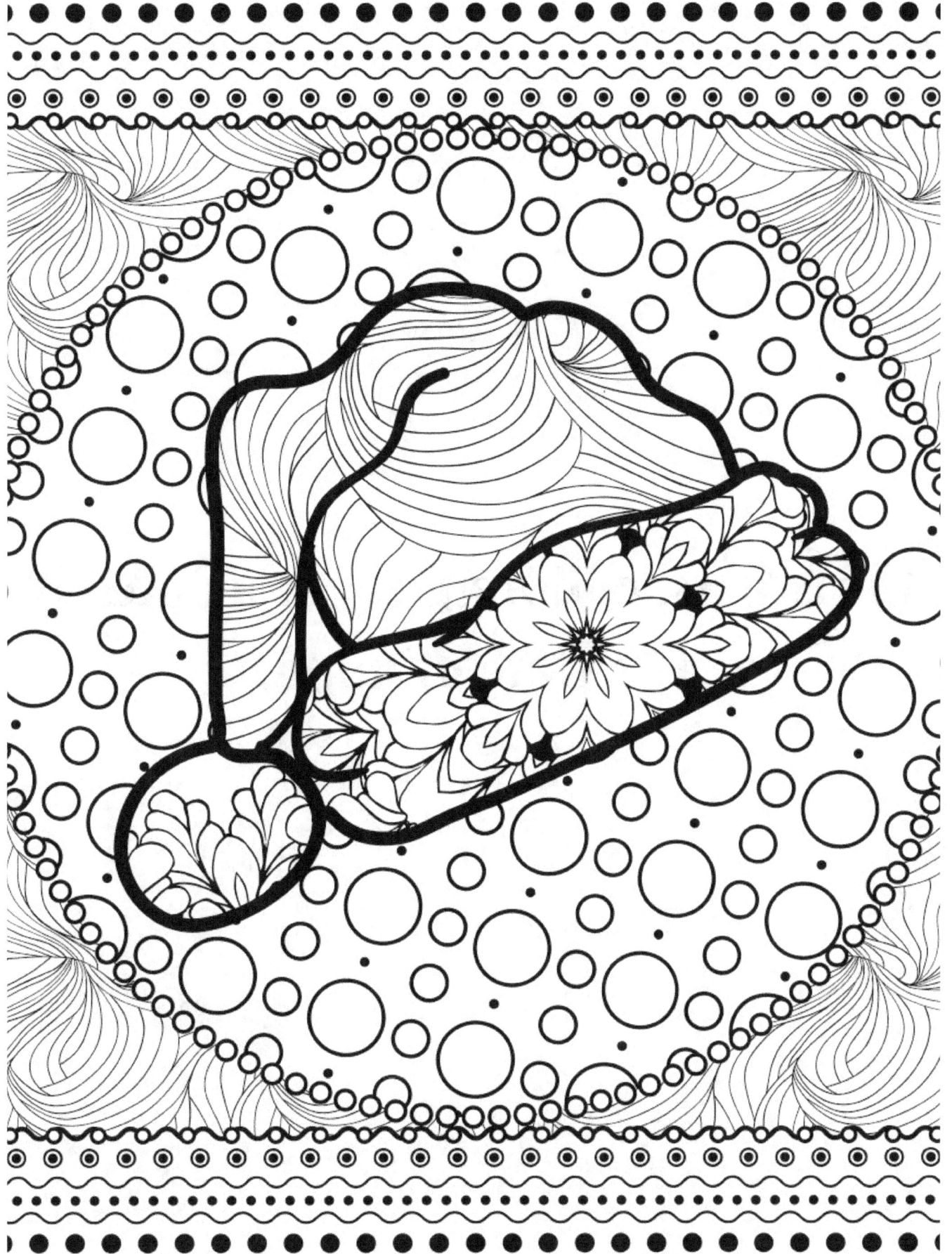

Christmas, children, is not a date. It is a state of mind.

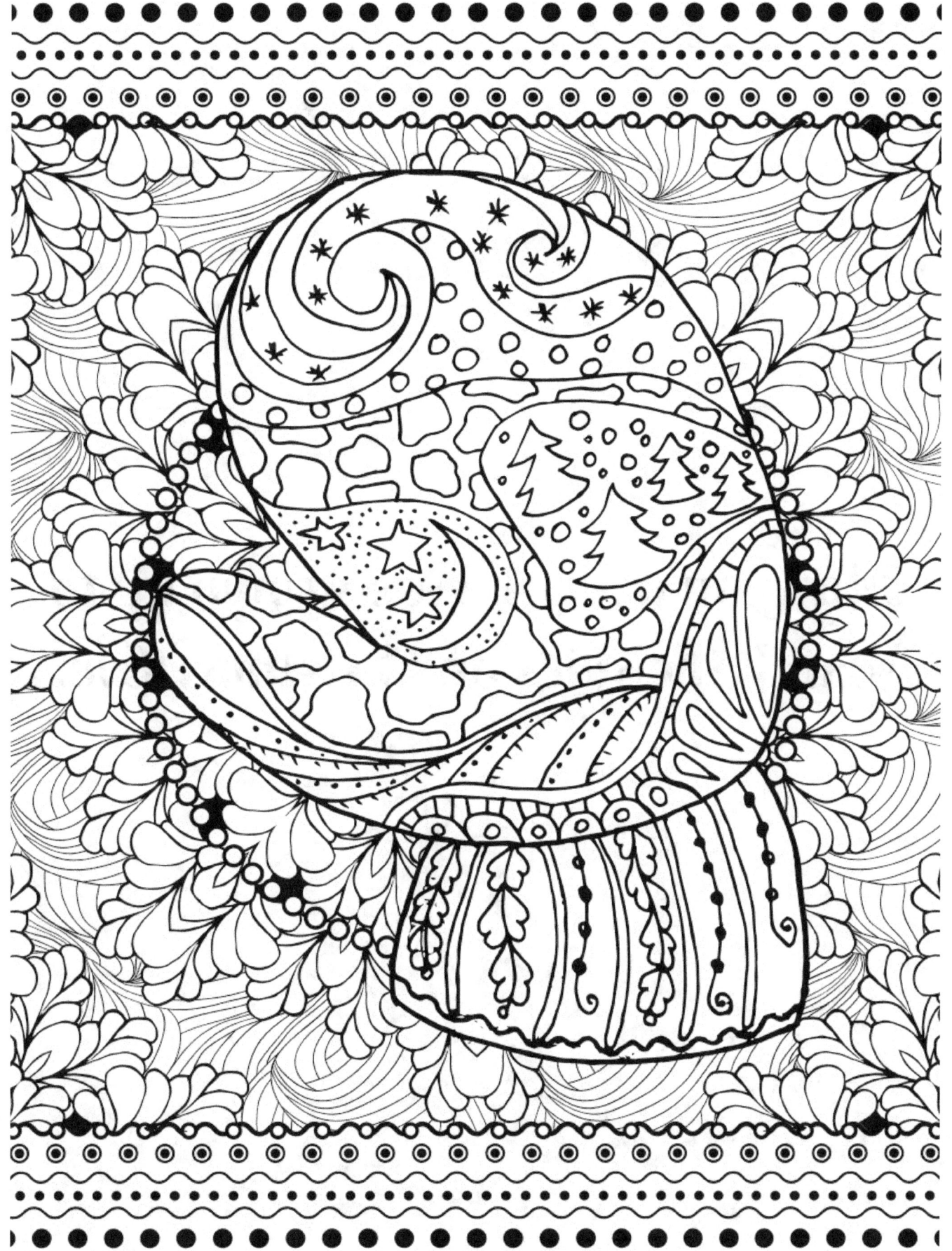

May you never be too grown up to search the skies on Christmas Eve.

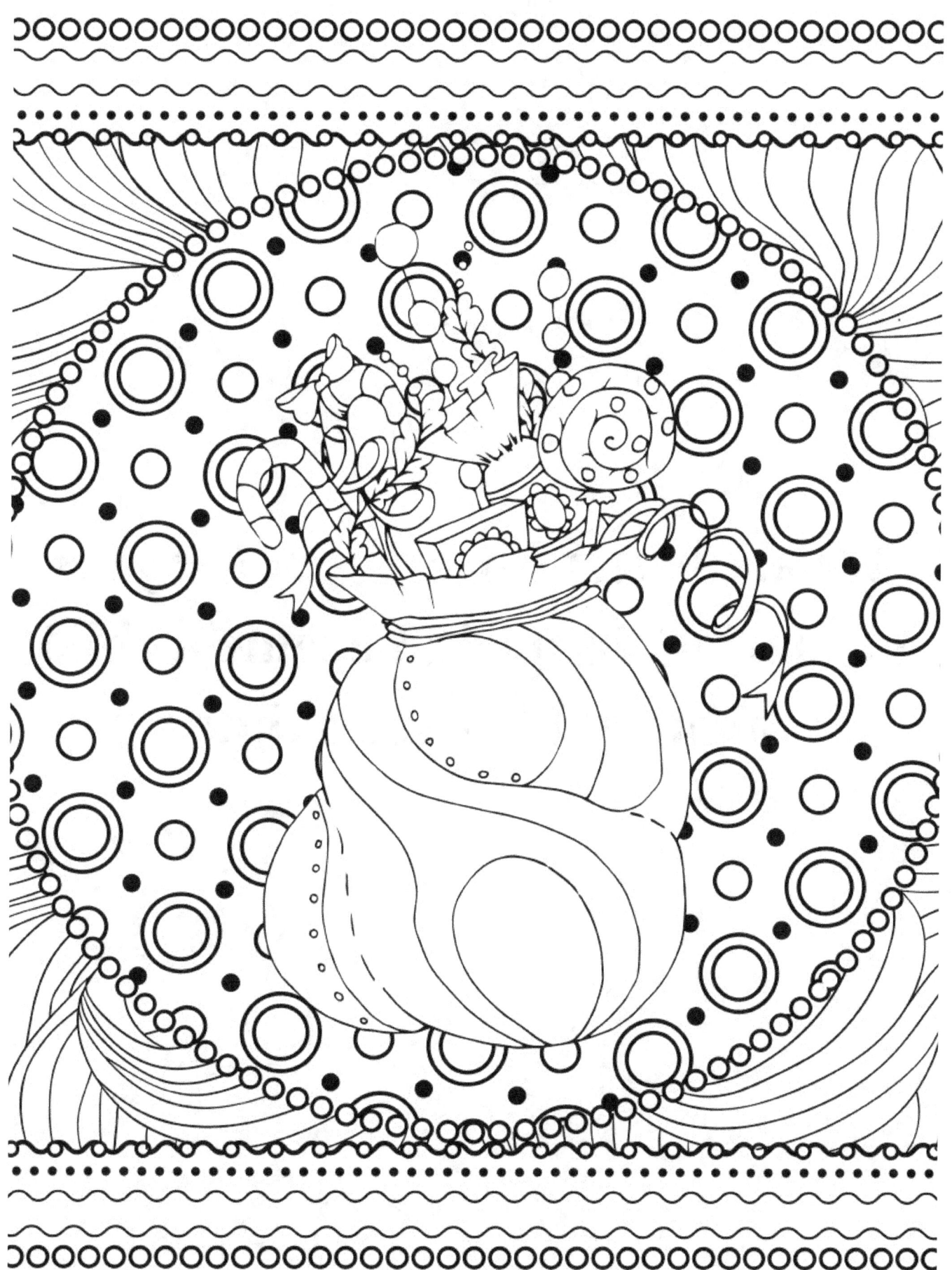

We are better throughout the year for having, in spirit, become a child again at Christmas time.

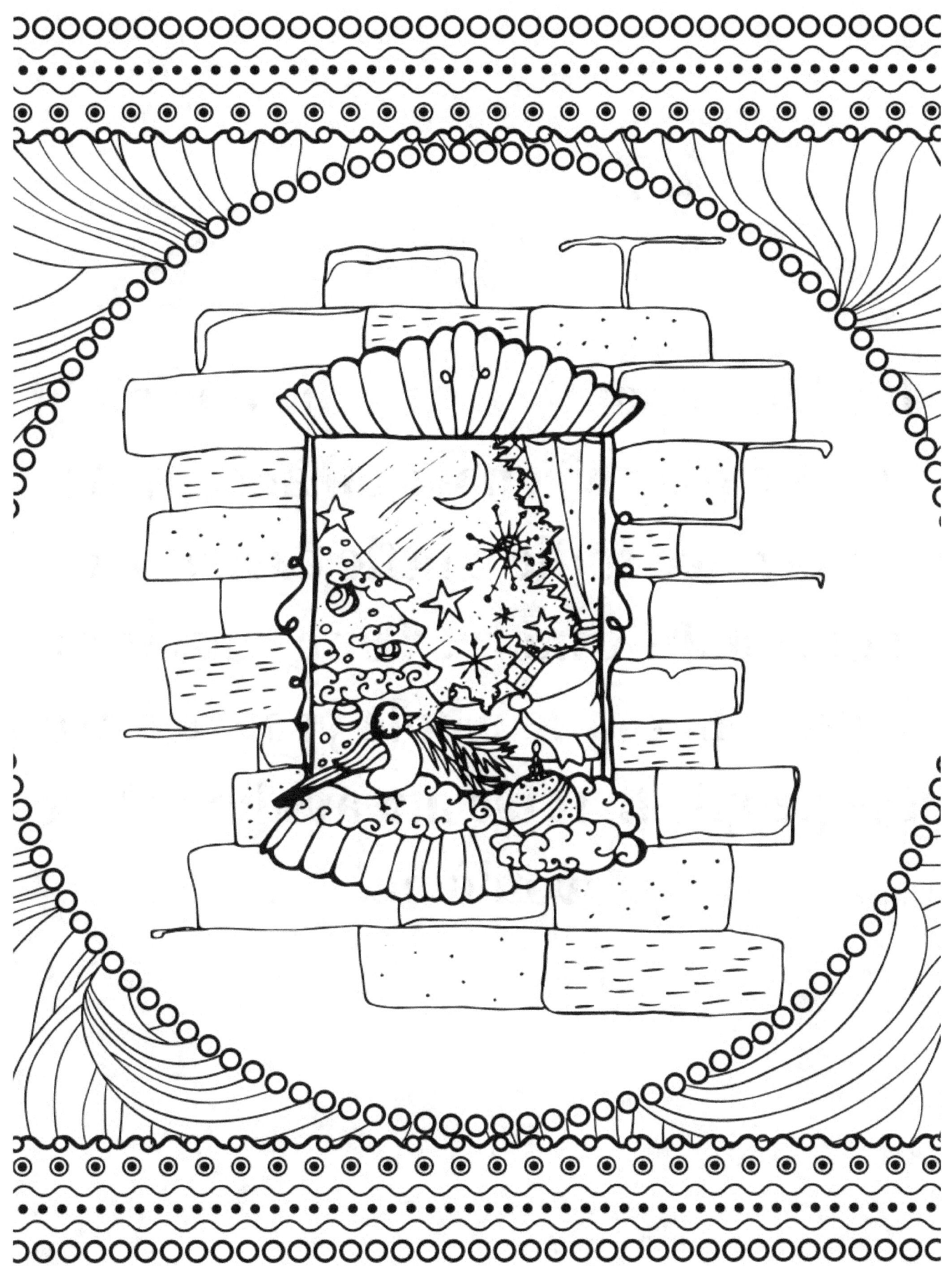

It's Christmas Eve. It's the one night of the year when we all act a little nicer, we smile a little easier, we cheer a little more. For a couple of hours out of the whole year, we are the people that we always hoped we would be.

Christmas is doing a little something extra for someone.

I wish we could put up some of the Christmas spirit in jars and open a jar of it every month.

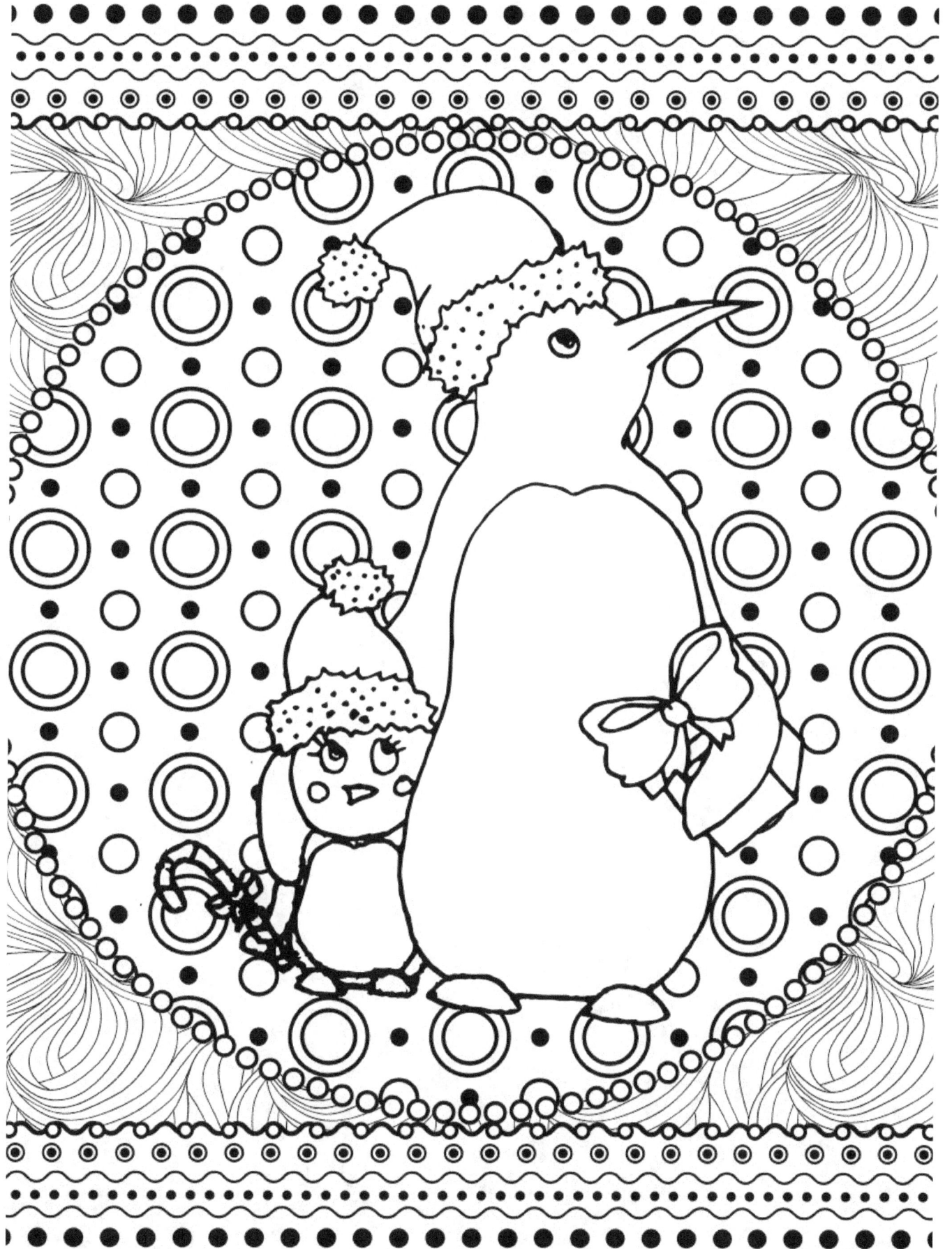

www.ingramcontent.com/pod-product-compliance
Lightning Source LLC
Chambersburg PA
CBHW081703220526
45466CB00009B/2861